THE POWER OF THE PEOPLE

THE DECLARATION OF INDEPENDENCE, THE CONSTITUTION, AND THE BILL OF RIGHTS

by Ellen Sutherland

Scott Foresman
is an imprint of

Glenview, Illinois • Boston, Massachusetts • Chandler, Arizona
Upper Saddle River, New Jersey

ISBN 13: 978-0-328-51645-2
ISBN 10:   0-328-51645-7

3 4 5 6 7 8 9 10 V0N4 13 12 11 10

What does the United States stand for? What do we value, and what do we want for our people? How do we know what our laws are? Two important and honored documents can tell us: the Declaration of Independence and the Constitution with its Bill of Rights. These documents were written a long time ago, but they have lasted to this day. Let's take a look at how and why they were written. That will help us understand why they are still so important to us today.

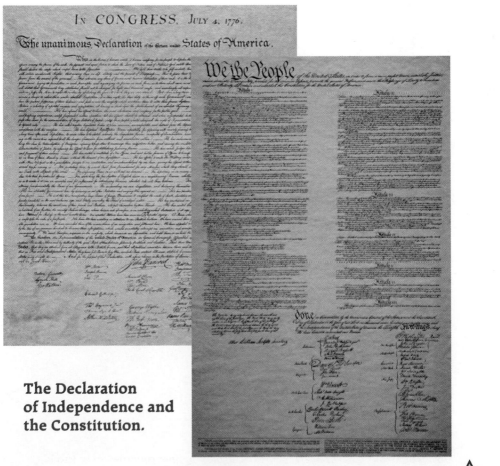

The Declaration
of Independence and
the Constitution.

Think of July 4, and you probably think of fireworks. July 4 is called Independence Day, and it dates back to 1776. That's the day the Declaration of Independence was signed in Philadelphia, Pennsylvania. But did you know that signing the Declaration of Independence was a dangerous and revolutionary act?

Let's go back in time to colonial America. At that time, Americans had been fighting their British rulers for more rights. They didn't like the high taxes they had to pay Britain.

Delegates at the Continental Congress

They also didn't like being told what to do by a country far away from them. Even so, most colonists didn't think the colonies would ever break from British rule.

But as British rule dragged on, the colonists began to think that the best thing to do was to form their own nation. A Continental Congress, comprised of **representatives** from each of the colonies, began to meet to discuss the problems with British rule. Each colony (except for Georgia, which joined later) appointed a delegation to the Congress.

This action made England angry. In late 1775, it granted Parliament **sovereignty** over the colonies. This meant the colonists could not govern themselves. This made the colonists furious.

So, the colonists formed an army. In May of 1776, the Continental Congress advised each of the colonies to adopt a government of its own choosing. On June 7, 1776, Virginia made a motion to Congress that all states be declared independent from England.

People were shocked! Should they really do this? What would England do?

Quickly, colonial leaders Thomas Jefferson, John Adams, Benjamin Franklin, Roger Sherman, and Robert R. Livingston began to prepare

a special document. It would outline reasons the colonies should separate from England and declare independence. The men worked on the document for the month of June.

Benjamin Franklin and Thomas Jefferson

Thomas Jefferson, John Adams, Benjamin Franklin, Roger Sherman, and Robert R. Livingston worked on the Declaration of Independence.

Thomas Jefferson wrote much of the Declaration of Independence. His fellow committee members asked him to write the first draft. When Jefferson was finished, they made minor changes. The Declaration was written on parchment, and it had two parts. First was a preamble, or introduction. This listed the rights of every man. Second was a list of the wrongs they felt the King of England had committed against them.

By July 1, the men were ready to present the document to the Second Continental Congress.

The Congress **unanimously** adopted the Declaration on July 4,1776—the day we now celebrate as Independence Day.

"Declaration of Independence, 4 July, 1776" by John Trumbull ca. 1786–1819.

The signing of the Declaration of Independence, as shown in a painting by John Trumbull

John Adams would later say that he did not think the Declaration of Independence was really unique in its **politics**. He said that it borrowed heavily from the works of the philosopher John Locke. The Declaration also had a lot in common with Thomas Paine's pamphlet *Common Sense*. Paine, a political thinker and writer, had also argued passionately for independence from England.

Still, this was the first time that a whole people had asserted their right to choose a government for themselves.

John Locke and Thomas Paine

"Thomas Paine" by John Wesley Jarvis ca. 1806.

9

People come from all over the world to view the Declaration of Independence at the National Archives.

Some historians refer to the signing of the Declaration of Independence as the "Miracle of Philadelphia." Think about it: thirteen separate and very different colonies had sent representatives to the Second Continental Congress in Philadelphia. There, they had managed to agree on a vision for our new nation.

Today, you can visit the site of the signing—the former Pennsylvania State House, now known as Independence Hall. You can also see the original Declaration at the National Archives in Washington, D.C.

In many ways, the Declaration of Independence set the stage for our Constitution. The Constitution is the highest law in the United States. All other laws come from it. The Constitution describes how our government works. It also explains the rights and **responsibilities** enjoyed by each citizen. If it weren't for our Constitution, we wouldn't have the President, or Congress, or the Supreme Court.

The U.S. Constitution uses simple language to describe our government. It is the oldest written set of governing principles for the United States in use today. It is also short, at about 4,500 words! The Constitution is called a "living document." That means that it was designed to work today as well as in the 1700s.

It's not easy to make changes to the Constitution. The Constitution can only be changed by **amendments** that have been approved by a majority of the states. Think about this: thousands of amendments have been proposed, but just twenty-seven amendments have been approved!

The first ten of these amendments are considered special and are known as the Bill of Rights.

The Constitution can be amended, or changed. Sometimes people work to change it or protest a change they don't want.

The U.S. Constitution was written in 1787, more than 200 years ago. If some of its ideas sound familiar, that's because many of its authors were the same people who wrote the Declaration of Independence.

Between May and September of 1787, a Federal Constitutional Convention met in Philadelphia to change the Articles of **Confederation**, a document that outlined our government. Some didn't really like this document because it gave most of the power to the states and little to the central government. Congress had to depend on the states for its funding.

The Assembly Room in Independence Hall

It quickly became clear that it would be too difficult to change this document. Instead, a new one would have to be written. George Washington, Benjamin Franklin, and James Madison worked to decide what this new document should cover.

Gouveneur Morris is probably responsible for how the Constitution sounds. But Jacob Shallus, a Pennsylvania General Assembly clerk, is credited with actually writing down the words. He did it for just $30.

James Madison, the "father of the Constitution"

The Constitutional Convention was attended by representatives from each of the thirteen states (except Rhode Island). They met in secret during the hot summer in the Pennsylvania State House.

To create the document, they discussed, argued, and **compromised** for six months. James Madison's "Virginia Plan" called for a state and national government. The more people a state had, the more representatives it sent to the national government. If Madison's plan passed, the small states would have almost no say! The small states drew up their own plan, "The New Jersey Plan." This plan gave each state the same number of representatives.

After much arguing, Connecticut suggested "The Great Compromise." This created a legislature that was **bicameral**, or made up of two rooms, or chambers. This government had a Senate and a House of Representatives. Each state had two senators, but the number of representatives each state sent to the House would be based on population.

The Constitution had to be approved, or **ratified**, by the people. Nine of the thirteen states had to approve it. And they did!

"Signing of the United States Constitution" by Junius Brutus Stearns, 1856.

Delegates argued over the writing of the Constitution, but in the end, they compromised.

The nine states that ratified the Constitution were Delaware, Pennsylvania, New Jersey, Georgia, Connecticut, Massachusetts, Maryland, South Carolina, and then, later, New Hampshire. But the writers of the Constitution wanted every state to agree to it.

So they decided to advertise! Alexander Hamilton, John Jay, and James Madison published essays about the Constitution in New York newspapers. A collection of these essays was later published and became known as *The Federalist Papers*.

The signing of the Constitution

It took a long time to get all the states to ratify the Constitution. One reason was that it didn't contain a Bill of Rights—a description of all the rights that belong to the people. Many of the writers of the Constitution had worried that if they listed citizens' rights, they might actually be limiting them. But because everyone was so concerned, the writers promised to add a Bill of Rights once the new government was in place.

On September 25, 1789, the First Congress of the United States proposed to the state legislatures an amendment, or change, to the Constitution. There were twelve Articles. Articles 3 through 12 were turned into separate amendments and ratified on December 15, 1791. These ten amendments became known as the Bill of Rights. The remaining two Articles were ratified later.

The Bill of Rights

These amendments guarantee American citizens certain rights and freedoms. We have freedom of religion and speech. We can hold meetings, and we have freedom of the press.

The rights guaranteed by the Bill of Rights, however, are not necessarily absolute or without limits or restrictions. The wording of the original amendments has led to lots of political debate. For example, many people are not happy with the Second Amendment's "right to bear arms." This gives people the right to keep firearms. Those against this amendment feel it leads to more violence in today's society.

Our right to free speech is one of the amendments in the Bill of Rights.

As our country grew and changed, far-reaching amendments were added. One of them was the 19th Amendment. This gave women the right to vote.

Our Constitution really is a living document. It was designed to meet the needs of a new and growing country. It continues to meet the needs of our country today.

Women fought hard for the right to vote.

Now Try This

Establishing a New Nation

Have you ever wondered what it would be like to start your own country—or just a place to call your own? What kind of place do you want to claim as your own? Brainstorm with a group and then work together to describe it. What are the principles behind it? What rules and ideas might you use to run it?

Write your ideas down, debate their various merits, and then agree on a set of rules, or a constitution.

Working to build a new nation is hard work.

1. After you are all in agreement about what you want, write a constitution for your new government. Use reference materials and primary source documents as a model. Give the leaders responsibilities and the citizens rights. You will probably have to debate and compromise quite a bit.

2. Now for ratification. Who has to ratify the document, and how many votes will be needed? Will you vote or do a canvass (survey) of citizens? Remember, many documents or amendments have gotten to the point of ratification only to stop there. The process can be very challenging. You may have to go back and revise the document before you can get it ratified.

3. Once the document is ratified as a constitution, use your art skills to draw a map of your new nation. Give your new nation a name and a capital—the names can reflect important people or shared beliefs.

Glossary

amendments *n.* formal revisions to a document.

bicameral *adj.* composed of two legislative branches.

compromised *v.* settled by concessions, or agreements to give in part-way.

confederation *n.* a political union of persons, parties, or states.

politics *n.* the art or science of government or governing.

ratified *adj.* approved and given formal sanction to.

representatives *n.* delegates or agents acting on behalf of others.

responsibilities *n.* things for which one must be accountable.

sovereignty *n.* supremacy of authority or rule.

unanimously *adv.* in a manner reflecting complete agreement.